BETHLEHEM TOWN

Where Jesus Was Born

PATRICIA A. HOFFMAN

ILLUSTRATED BY NANCY MUNGER

CONCORDIA PUBLISHING HOUSE • SAINT LOUIS

For Maggie, with whom I love to share Christmas and Easter.

*Thank you, Helen and Chuck, Barbara and Ron,
and Delores, my Christmas and Easter friends.*

Long, long ago, when the time was just right,
The stars filled the sky on a quiet, still night.

The sky was filled with bright, shiny light,
And something so special happened that night.

In Bethlehem town God's plan would begin,
To save the world from death, devil, and sin.

Joseph and Mary began searching the town
For a place to sleep as the sun went down.

"No room!" they heard. "There just is no room!"
"But Mary," said Joseph, "will have a baby quite soon."

"No room," said the next man as he slammed shut the door.
"No room," said another. "No room," said one more.

"Please, sir," Joseph begged, "for my wife show some pity."
"I'm sorry," he said. "There's no room in the city."

"Wait!" said the innkeeper. "There might be a place.
In the stable, near the animals, we'll give her some space."

"Wait!" said the innkeeper. "There might be a place.
In the stable, near the animals, we'll give her some space."

"Please, sir," Joseph begged, "for my wife show some pity."
"I'm sorry," he said. "There's no room in the city."

"No room," said the next man as he slammed shut the door. "No room," said another. "No room," said one more.

"No room!" they heard. "There just is no room!"

"But Mary," said Joseph, "will have a baby quite soon."

Joseph and Mary began searching the town
For a place to sleep as the sun went down.

In Bethlehem town God's plan would begin,
To save the world from death, devil, and sin.

To the city of David, Mary and Joseph came,
So on the king's list they could write their names.

Mary and Joseph were ending a journey.
From Nazareth town they had come in a hurry.

The sky was filled with bright, shiny light,
And something so special happened that night.

L

ong, long ago, when the time was just right,
The stars filled the sky on a quiet, still night.

For Maggie, with whom I love to share Christmas and Easter.

Thank you, Helen and Chuck, Barbara and Ron,
and Delores, my Christmas and Easter friends.

BETHLEHEM TOWN

Where Jesus Was Born

PATRICIA A. HOFFMAN

ILLUSTRATED BY NANCY MUNGER

CONCORDIA PUBLISHING HOUSE • SAINT LOUIS